CGP

GCSE

Mathematics

WJEC Modular

For **New GCSE** courses starting from **Sept '10**

Answer Book

Higher Level

W0010157

Answers: P.1 — P.7

Unit One
Rounding Numbers P.1

Q1
a) 62.2
b) 62.19
c) 62.194
d) 19.62433
e) 6.300
f) 3.142

Q2
a) 1330
b) 1330
c) 1329.6
d) 100
e) 0.02
f) 0.02469

Q3
a) 457.0
b) 456.99
c) 456.987
d) 457
e) 460
f) 500

Q4 23 kg

Q5 £5.07

Q6 235 miles

Q7 £19

Q8 £4.77

Q9 235 cm

Calculation Bounds P.2-P.3

Q1 4.5 m to 5.5 m

Q2
a) 142.465 kg
b) 142.455 kg

Q3
a) 95 g
b) Upper bound = 97.5 g, lower bound = 92.5 g.
c) No, since the lower bound for the electronic scales is 97.5 g, which is greater than the upper bound for the scales in part a).

Q4
a) Perimeter = 2(12 + 4) = 32 cm. Maximum possible error = 4 × 0.1 cm = 0.4 cm.
b) Maximum possible error in P is $2(x + y)$.

Q5
a) Upper bound = 945, lower bound = 935.
b) Upper bound = 5.565, lower bound = 5.555.
c) To find the upper bound for R, divide the upper bound for S by the lower bound for T;
945 ÷ 5.555 = 170.117...
To find the lower bound for R, divide the lower bound for S by the upper bound for T;
935 ÷ 5.565 = 168.014...
d) 940 ÷ 5.56 = 170 (to 2 s.f., as both upper and lower bound agree to 2 s.f.).

Q6 At least 18.2 m²

Q7 The upper bound for the distance is 100.5 m. The lower bound for the time is 10.25 s. Therefore the maximum value of Vince's average speed is 100.5 ÷ 10.25 = 9.805 m/s.

Q8 The upper bound for the distance is 127.5 km. The lower bound for the time is 1 hour and 45 minutes = 1.75 hours. The maximum value of the average speed is 127.5 ÷ 1.75 = 72.857... km/hour.

Q9
a) Upper bound = 5 minutes 32.5 seconds, lower bound = 5 minutes 27.5 seconds.
b) The lower bound for Jimmy's time is 5 minutes 25 seconds, which is lower than the lower bound for Douglas' time (5 minutes 25.5 seconds).

Calculator Buttons P.4

Q1
a) 1
b) 4
c) 121
d) 256
e) 1
f) 900
g) 25
h) 1 000 000
i) 0

Q2
a) 4
b) 6
c) 17
d) 0
e) 60
f) 20
g) 1.732 (to 3 d.p.)
h) 2.646 (to 3 d.p.)
i) 5.477 (to 3 d.p.)

Q3
a) 1
b) 0
c) 7
d) 10
e) 3
f) –3
g) –4
h) –1.710 (to 3 d.p.)

Q4
a) 8.4
b) 0.622 (3 s.f.)
c) 0.080 (3 s.f.)

Q5
a) 2
b) 1
c) 0.333 (3 d.p.)
d) 29.867 (3 d.p.)
e) 0.353 (3 d.p.)
f) 0.0729 (3 s.f.)

Q6
a) 1
b) 1 048 576
c) 1 048 576
d) 9.870 (3 d.p.)
e) 0.5
f) 59 049
g) 26 742 (5 s.f.)

Fractions P.5

Q1
a) 1/12
b) 1/4
c) 2/3

Q2
a) 3/4 of the programme
b) 5/8 of the programme
c) 1/8 of the programme

Q3 3/5 of the kitchen staff are girls. 2/5 of the employees are boys.

Q4 7/30 of those asked had no opinion.

Q5
a) 12/30 = 2/5
b) 6 days

Q6
a) Each box will hold 16 sandwiches. So 5 boxes will be needed for 80 sandwiches.
b) 25 inches tall

Percentages P.6-P.7

Q1 £351.33

Q2 £244.40

Q3 23 028

Q4 a) £4275   b) £6840

Q5 Car 1 costs £8495 – (0.15 × £8495) = £8495 – £1274.25 = £7220.75.
Car 2 costs £8195 – (0.12 × £8195) = £8195 – £983.40 = £7211.60.
So car 2 is the cheapest.

Q6 a) £5980   b) £5501.60

Q7 £152.75, So NO, he couldn't afford it.

Q8 31%

Q9 13%

Q10 1.6%

Q11 500%

Q12 38%

Q13 £80

Q14
a) 300
b) 4 whole years

Q15 After four years, the savings at Burnley and Brighouse would be worth:
1200(1 + 4.5/100)⁴ = £1431
After four years, the savings at Natvest would be worth:
1200 + (1200(5.5/100 × 4)) = £1464
So the best account to choose is the Natvest account.

Q16 £10 400

Answers: P.8 — P.14

Speed and Density P.8

Q1 **a)** 98.9 mph (to 3 s.f.)
  b) 72.56 seconds
  c) 99.2 mph (to 3 s.f.)

Q2 **a)** 2.77 + 1.96 + 0.6 = 5.33 hrs
   (to 3 s.f.) = 5 hours 20 mins
  b) 250 miles
  c) 46.9 mph (to 3 s.f.)

Q3 The first athlete ran at 16000 ÷ (60 × 60) = 4.44 m/s, so was faster than the second athlete (at 4 m/s). The first athlete would take 37.5 mins to run 10 km; the second would take 41.7 mins.

Q4 **a)** 487.5 km
  b) 920.8 km
  c) 497 km/h

Q5 34.71 g

Q6 20968 cm^3

Q7 Vol. = 5000 cm^3 = 5 litres

Conversion Graphs P.9

Q1 **a)** £5
  b) £9.50
  c) £17
  d) No (Each 4.5 mile journey costs more than £8)

Q2 **a)** 12-13 miles
  b) 43-44 miles
  c) 56-57 miles

Q3 **a)** 63-65 km
  b) 15-17 km
  c) 47-49 km

Conversion Factors and Units P.10-P.11

Q1 **a)** 200 cm   **i)** 6000 mm
  b) 33 mm   **j)** 2000 kg
  c) 4000 g   **k)** 3 kg
  d) 0.6 kg   **l)** 86 mm
  e) 0.65 km   **m)** 0.55 tonnes
  f) 9000 g   **n)** 354 cm
  g) 0.007 kg   **o)** 7 mm
  h) 0.95 kg

Q2 147 kg × 2.2 = 323.4 lbs (1 d.p.)

Q3 14 gallons = 14 × 4.5 = 63 litres

Q4 59.1 kg

Q5 Barry cycled 30 miles = 30 × 1.6 = 48 km. So Barbara cycled furthest.

Q6 **a)** 11 in = 11 × 2.5 = 27.5 cm
  b) 275 mm

Q7 **a)** 21 feet = 21 × 12 = 252 in
  b) 21 feet = 21 ÷ 3 = 7 yd
  c) 21 feet = 21 × 0.3 = 6.3 m
  d) 6.3 m = 630 cm
  e) 630 cm = 6300 mm
  f) 6.3 m = 0.0063 km

Q8 5 lb = 5 ÷ 2.2 = 2.3 kg. So Dick needs to buy 3 bags of sugar.

Q9 **a)** £148.65   **g)** £81.50
  b) £62.19   **h)** £13.51
  c) £679.18   **i)** £272.65
  d) £100   **j)** £307.25
  e) £1.36   **k)** £408.16
  f) £795.92   **l)** £0.68

Q10 **a)** 60 kg = 60 × 2.2 = 132 lbs
  b) 132 lbs = 132 × 16 = 2112 oz.
  c) 0.059 t = 59 kg, so Arnold can lift most.

Q11 **a)** £4.69
  b) £51.07

Q12 Beer in the hotel costs 4 × 0.568 = €2.27 per pint.
€2.27 ÷ 1.48 = £1.53
So the beer is better value in the hotel.

Q13 1 m = 1.1 yards, so 1 m^2 = (1.1 yd)^2 = 1.21 yd^2.
£10.80 per sq. m = £10.80 ÷ 1.21 = £8.93 per sq. yard.
So the fabric superstore is cheaper.

Scale Drawings and Bearings P.12

Q1 **a)** 20 000 cm = 200 m
  b) 200 000 cm = 2000 m = 2 km
  c) 700 000 cm = 7000 m = 7 km
  d) 200 000 000 cm^2 = 20 000 m^2
   = 0.02 km^2

Q2 **a)** 1.67 m
  b) 33.3 cm
  c) 0.33 cm × 0.33 cm = 0.11 cm^2
  d) 0.056 cm^2

Q3 **a)** 232°-236°
  b) 132°-136°
  c) 278°-282°, 45°-49°, 225°-229°

Perimeter and Area P.13-P.14

Q1 Area 24 cm^2, perimeter 20 cm

Q2 Area 25 cm^2, perimeter 20 cm

Q3 **a)** Area = (4 × 4) − (1 × 2 + ½ × 3.14 ×1^2) + ½ × 3.14 × 2^2
   = 16 − 3.57 + 6.28
   = 18.7 m^2 (1 d.p.)
  b) Three 1 litre tins of paint are needed for two coats.
  c) Perimeter = 1 + 1 + (½ × 3.14 × 2) + 1 + 1 + 4 + (½ × 3.14 × 4) + 4
   = 12 + (3 × 3.14) = 21.4 m (1 d.p.)

Q4 **a)** l = 24, w = 12, area = 288 m^2
  b) 1 Carpet tile = 0.50 × 0.50
   = 0.25 m^2
   So 288 m^2 ÷ 0.25 = 1152 tiles are required.
  c) £4.99 per m^2 => £4.99 for 4 tiles
   Total cost = (1152 ÷ 4) × 4.99
   = £1437.12

Q5 Area = 120 cm^2

Q6 Each square = 0.6 m × 0.6 m = 0.36 m^2.
Total area of material = 6 × 0.36 = 2.16 m^2.

Q7 Perimeter = 4 × $\sqrt{9000}$
= 379.47 m (2 d.p.)
Natasha ran: 11 × 379.47
= 4200 m (to nearest 100 m)

Q8 **a)** Area = area of a full circle radius 10 cm. A = πr^2 = 3.14 × 10^2
   = 314 cm^2.
   Circumference = π × D = 3.14 × 20 = 62.8 cm. Perimeter = 62.8 + 20 = 82.8 cm
  b) Area = (area of a full circle radius 15 cm) + (area of a rectangle 15 × 30 cm) = (π × 15^2) + (15 × 30)
   = 1156.5 cm^2.
   Perimeter = (Circumference of a full circle radius 15 cm) + 15 +15 (two shorter sides of rectangle) = (π × 30) + 30 = 124.2 cm.
  c) Area = Outer semi circle − Inner semi circle = 510.25 m^2.
   Perimeter = ½ Circumference of larger + ½ Circumference of inner + 5 + 5 = ½ × π × 70 + ½ × π × 60 + 10
   = 214.1 m.

Q9 80/360 × π5^2 = 17.45 cm^2

Q10 Area of larger triangle = ½ × 14.4 × 10 = 72 cm^2.
Area of inner triangle = ½ × 5.76 × 4 = 11.52 cm^2.
Area of metal used for a bracket = 72 − 11.52 = 60.48 cm^2.
No, the fixing will not take the weight of the bracket.

Q11 T_1: ½ × 8 × 16 = 64 m²
Tr_1: ½ × 8 × (8 + 16) = 96 m²
Tr_2: ½ × 4 × (8 + 12) = 40 m²
T_2: ½ × 8 × 12 = 48 m²
Total area of glass sculpture = 248 m²

Q12 a) Area of each isosceles triangle = ½
× 2.3 × 3.2 = 3.68 m²
b) Area of each side =
3.4 × 4 = 13.6 m²
Groundsheet = 2.3 × 4 = 9.2 m²
c) Total material = 2 × 3.68 + 9.2 +
2 × 13.6 = 43.8 m²

Q13

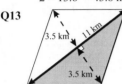

Area = area of two triangles:
= 2(½ × base x height)
= 2(½ × 11 × 3.5) = 38.5 km².

Volume P.15-P.16

Q1 a) $\frac{1}{2}\pi(0.35)^2$ = 0.192 m²
b) 0.1924 × 3 = 0.577 m³

Q2 a) $\pi(2.5^2 - 2^2)$ = 7.07 m²
£16 × 7.07 = £113.12 = £110 to
nearest £10.
b) Volume = $\pi(2)^2 \times 0.50$ = 6.28 m³
so use 6.28 × 15 = 94 ml treatment
to the nearest ml.

Q3 a) Volume Cube = Volume Cylinder
$10^3 = \pi r^2 \times 10$ so $r^2 = \frac{10^2}{\pi}$,
$r = 5.64$ cm
b) S.A. of cylinder = $2\pi rh + 2\pi r^2$ =
2π × 5.64... × 10 + 2π × (5.64...)²
= 554.49 cm².

Q4 a) $\pi(5)^2(16)$ = 1257 cm³
b) $\pi(5)^2h = 600$
$h = \frac{600}{25\pi}$ = 7.64 cm

Q5 $(3)(3)(0.5) - \pi(0.7)^2(0.5)$ = 3.73 cm³

Q6 $(\pi \times(2)^2 \times 110)$ +
(½(14 + 20) × 6 × 20) = 3422.30 cm³
2 × 3422.30 = 6844.60 cm³ = 6.84 l

Q7 a) (60)(30) + (30)(120) = 5400 cm²
b) 5400 × 100 = 540000 cm³ =
0.54 m³

Q8 1 panel on roof = ½AB × $\frac{5}{2}$
= 1.25 × 2.5 = 3.125 m²
Front of greenhouse = (2.5 × 4) + (½
× 4 × 1.5) = 13 m²
Total = 3.125 + 13 = 16.125 m²

Q9 Volume of ice cream
$= \frac{1}{3}\pi(R^2H - r^2h) + \frac{1}{2}(\frac{4}{3}\pi R^3)$
$= \frac{1}{3}\pi(2.5^2 \times 10 - 1^2 \times 4)$
$+ \frac{1}{2}(\frac{4}{3}\pi \times 2.5^3)$
= 93.99 cm³ of ice cream.

Q10 Vol. increase is a cylinder of height
4.5 cm. So vol. increase =
$\pi(5)^2 \times 4.5$ = 353.4 cm³.
Volume of each ball bearing = $\frac{353.4}{200}$
= 1.767 cm³
$\frac{4}{3}\pi r^3 = 1.767 \Rightarrow r = 0.75$ cm

Collecting Data P.17

Q1 a) E.g. the question is vague/
subjective – "very often" can
mean different things to different
people.
b) Any sensible answer, e.g. "How
many times a week do you visit
the school canteen?"

Q2 E.g. the question isn't relevant to
what the council wants to find out.

Q3 a) Unsuitable — e.g. people may
like every one of the desserts,
and this wouldn't tell you which
was their favourite.
b) Unsuitable — e.g. the question is
not relevant.
c) Suitable — it is the only one
which will always tell you which
of the five desserts people like
the most.
d) Unsuitable — e.g. question is
too vague, so people may give
answers which are not on the list
of desserts.
e) Unsuitable — e.g. people's
favourite dessert may not be on
the list, so you wouldn't find
out which they prefer out of the
desserts on the list.

Q4 a) E.g.

Café Questionnaire
1) Please tick the box to show how often you visit the café:
daily ☐ weekly ☐ fortnightly ☐ monthly ☐ less than monthly ☐
2) Please tick the box to show how often you buy cola:
daily ☐ weekly ☐ fortnightly ☐ monthly ☐ less than monthly ☐

b) She will miss out the people who
just buy drinks from the hot and
cold drinks machines.

Mean, Median, Mode and Range P.18-P.19

Q1 3 tries

Q2 mean = 1.333 (to 3 dp)
median = 1.5
mode = 2
range = 11

Q3 a) mean = £12,944, or £13,000 to the
nearest £500
median = £12,000
mode = £7,500
b) mode
c) E.g. mean — they should use the
highest value to attract people to the
job.

Q4 a) 0 minutes
b) 0 minutes
c) 0 minutes
d) No, according to the raw data.

Q5 73.5 kg

Q6 20 kg

Q7 97%

Q8 a) 22   **b)** 74

Q9 a) 3.5
b) 3.5   **c)** 5

Q10 a) Both spend a mean of 2 hours.
b) The range for Jim is 3 hours and for
Bob is 2 hours.
c) The amount of TV that Jim watches
each night is more variable than the
amount that Bob watches.

Q11 a) 1 day
b) 2 days
c) The statement is true according to the
data.

Q12 a) mode
b) median   **c)** mean

Answers: P.20 — P.23

Frequency Tables P.20-P.21

Q1 a) 12   **b)** 12

Q2 a)

Subject	M	E	F	A	S
Frequency	5	7	3	4	6

b) 36 French lessons

c) English

Q3

Length (m)	4 and under	6	8	10	12	14 and over
Frequency	3	5	6	4	1	1

a) 8 m

b) 8 m   **c)** 14 m

Q4

Weight (kg)	Frequency	Weight × Frequency
51	40	2040
52	30	1560
53	45	2385
54	10	540
55	5	275

a) 52 kg

b) 53 kg

c) 52 kg (to nearest kg)

Q5 mean = 3.75

mode = 3

median = 4

Q6 a) 4

b) 3   **c)** 3.2 (to 1 dp)

Q7 a) i) False, mode is 8.

ii) False, they are equal.

iii) True

b) iv)

Charts and Graphs P.22

Q1 a) 35

b) 52

c) 9

d) 21

Q2 a) E.g. tally chart

Level of skier	No.
Beginner	|||| |||
Intermediate	|||| ||||
Good	||||
Very good	|||
Racer	|||

b) E.g. bar chart

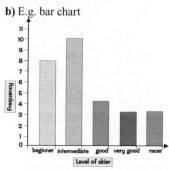

c) Most common type of skier is Intermediate.

Q3 Complaints have not "tailed off" - they have remained the same (approx 10,850) per month. The number of complaints is not increasing but there are still 10,850 per month, every month. The products cannot possibly be getting made to a higher quality if the complaints remain the same each month.

Pie Charts P.23

Q1 $\frac{360°}{100} = 3.6°$ per gram

Carbohydrate	3.6 × 35 = 126°
Protein	3.6 × 15 = 54°
Fat	3.6 × 10 = 36°
Magical Fairy Dust	3.6 × 40 = 144°

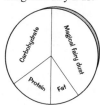

Q2 Sherrington 380,000 = 147° (approx)

2600 visitors = 1°

So, to the nearest 10,000:

Brompton = 2600 × 119° ≈ 310,000

Barny = 2600 × 44° ≈ 110,000

Livsea = 2600 × 50° ≈ 130,000

Q3 Part **c)**

Q4 It's not possible to tell whether more people voted for the Green Party in 2009, because you can't tell how many people voted in either election.

Answers: P.24 — P.29

Unit 2
Written Multiplication and Division P.24

Q1 **a)** 46   **e)** 5016
      b) 675   **f)** 10738
      c) 2730   **g)** 18849
      d) 1764   **h)** 44891

Q2 **a)** 278   **d)** 125   **g)** 48
      b) 129   **e)** 35   **h)** 41.5
      c) 117   **f)** 56   **i)** 47.5

Q3 **a)** 24.8   **c)** 14.25   **e)** 368.2
      b) 43   **d)** 13.24   **f)** 0.3276

Q4 **a)** 6.8   **d)** 3.68   **g)** 2.15
      b) 5.3   **e)** 30.4   **h)** 16.8
      c) 7.45   **f)** 2.7   **i)** 39.2

Estimating P.25

Q1 **a)** $6500 \times 2 = 13\,000$
      b) $8000 \times 1.5 = 12\,000$
      c) $40 \times 1.5 \times 5 = 300$
      d) $45 \div 9 = 5$
      e) $35\,000 \div 7000 = 5$
      f) $\frac{55 \times 20}{10} = 55 \times 2 = 110$
      g) $7000 \times 2 = 14\,000$
      h) $100 \times 2.5 \times 2 = 500$
      i) $20 \times 20 \times 20 = 8000$
      j) $8000 \div 80 = 100$
      k) $62\,000 \div 1000 = 62$
      l) $3 \div 3 = 1$

Q2 Approximately $15\,000 - (1500 + 2500 + 1500 + 1500 + 3000) = 5000$

Q3
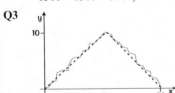

Area under the graph ≈ area of triangle = $\frac{1}{2} \times 30 \times 10 = 150$

Q4 **a)** $4 \times 7 = 28$ days
      b) As 1436 is approximately 1500, and 28 is approximately 30, the average is approximately:
      $1500 \div 30 = 50$ tins

Q5 **a)** 39 m^2 **b)** 3 tins

Q6 Mark's tank is approximately 4500 cm^3, so it won't be big enough.

Types of Number P.26

Q1 3

Q2 the third cube number (27)

Q3 **a)** 17, 19, 23, 29
      b) 81, 121, 169, 225
      c) 216, 512, 1000, 1728

Q4 **a)** 2
      b) e.g. 29
      c) 19
      d) 19 and 2
      e) e.g. 1 or 25

Q5 **a)**

1	②	③	4	⑤	6	⑦	8	9	10
⑪	12	⑬	14	15	16	⑰	18	⑲	20
21	22	㉓	24	25	26	27	28	㉙	30
㉛	32	33	34	35	36	㊲	38	39	40
㊶	42	㊸	44	45	46	㊲	48	49	50
51	52	㊳	54	55	56	57	58	㊴	60
㊶	62	63	64	65	66	㊲	68	69	70
㊱	72	㊳	74	75	76	77	78	㊲	80
81	82	㊳	84	85	86	87	88	㊲	90
91	92	㊳	94	95	96	㊲	98	99	100

      b) 3 of: 11 (11), 13 (31), 17 (71), 37 (73), 79 (97)
      c) e.g. 3 is a factor of 27

Q6 There's just one: 2 is the only even prime.

Multiples, Factors and Prime Factors P.27-P.28

Q1 **a)** 12
      b) 3
      c) 1, 9
      d) 1, 3, 9
      e) $P = 12, Q = 6$

Q2 Any 5 of:
      2 groups of 24, 3 groups of 16,
      4 groups of 12, 6 groups of 8,
      8 groups of 6, 12 groups of 4,
      16 groups of 3, 24 groups of 2.

Q3 The Conversational French and Woodturning classes both have a prime number of pupils and so cannot be divided into equal groups.

Q4 **a)** 1, 8, 27, 64, 125
      b) 8, 64
      c) 27
      d) 8, 64
      e) 125

Q5 **a)** 2×3^2
      b) $2^2 \times 5 \times 7$
      c) 47

Q6 **a)** 2, 3, 5, 7, 11
      b) 28
      c) $2^2 \times 7$

Q7 **a)** 1, 3, 5, 7, 9
      b) 25
      c) 5^2

Q8 **a)** 495
      b) $3 \times 5 \times 11$

Q9 **a)** $50 \times 25 \times 16 = 20{,}000 \text{ cm}^3$
      b) $2^5 \times 5^4$
      c) 200. It is not enough to divide the large volume by the smaller volume as the shapes of the blocks are important too. It is possible to fit $16 \div 4 = 4$ small blocks across the width, $50 \div 5 = 10$ small blocks along the length and $25 \div 5 = 5$ small blocks down the height of the large block. This enables Gordon to fit $4 \times 10 \times 5 = 200$ small blocks into the big block.

Q10 **a)** 680
       b) $2^2 \times 5 \times 17$
       c) $2 \times 5 \times 17$
       d) 5×17

Q11 42

LCM and HCF P.29

Q1 **a)** 6, 12, 18, 24, 30, 36, 42, 48, 54, 60
      b) 5, 10, 15, 20, 25, 30, 35, 40, 45, 50
      c) 30

Q2 **a)** 1, 2, 3, 5, 6, 10, 15, 30
      b) 1, 2, 3, 4, 6, 8, 12, 16, 24, 48
      c) 6

Q3 **a)** 20
      b) 10
      c) 2
      d) 15
      e) 15
      f) 5
      g) 32
      h) 16
      i) 16

Q4 **a)** 120
      b) 120
      c) 120
      d) 45
      e) 90
      f) 180
      g) 64
      h) 192
      i) 192

Q5 **a)** 7th June
      b) 16th June
      c) Sunday (1st July)
      d) Lars

Answers: P.30 — P.33

Roots and Reciprocals P.30

Q1 a) $\frac{1}{7}$ c) $\frac{8}{3}$
b) $\frac{1}{12}$ d) -2

Q2 a) $\frac{1}{20}$ c) 2
b) $\frac{1}{4}$ d) $\frac{2}{3}$

Q3 a) 2 and −2
b) 4 and −4
c) 3 and −3
d) 7 and −7
e) 5 and −5
f) 10 and −10
g) 12 and −12
h) 8 and −8
i) 9 and −9

Q4 a) 4
b) 10
c) 5
d) 6

Q5 7 cm

Q6 240 m

Powers P.31

Q1 a) 16
b) 1000
c) $3 \times 3 \times 3 \times 3 \times 3 = 243$
d) $4 \times 4 \times 4 \times 4 \times 4 \times 4 = 4096$
e) $1 \times 1 \times 1 \times 1 \times 1 \times 1 \times 1 \times 1 \times 1 = 1$
f) $5 \times 5 \times 5 \times 5 \times 5 \times 5 = 15\,625$

Q2 a) 2^8 (or 256)
b) 12^5 (or 248 832)
c) x^5
d) m^3
e) y^4
f) z^6

Q3 a) true b) true
c) false d) false
e) true f) false
g) false h) true
i) false j) true
k) true l) false

Q4 a) 3^{-3} d) 3^{-12}
b) 4^{25} e) 4^6
c) 10^{-13} f) 5^3

Q5 a) 12
b) 20
c) 1

Standard Index Form P.32

Q1 a) 35.6 b) 3560
c) 0.356 d) 35600
e) 8.2 f) 0.00082
g) 0.82 h) 0.0082
i) 1570 j) 0.157
k) 157000 l) 15.7

Q2 a) 2.56×10^0 b) 2.56×10
c) 2.56×10^{-1} d) 2.56×10^4
e) 9.52×10 f) 9.52×10^{-2}
g) 9.52×10^4 h) 9.52×10^{-4}
i) 4.2×10^3 j) 4.2×10^{-3}
k) 4.2×10 l) 4.2×10^2

Q3 a) 3.47×10^2 b) 7.3004×10
c) 5×10^0 d) 9.183×10^5
e) 1.5×10^7 f) 9.371×10^6
g) 7.5×10^{-5} h) 5×10^{-4}
i) 5.34×10^0 j) 6.2103×10^2
k) 1.49×10^4 l) 3×10^{-7}

Q4 6×10^{-3}

Q5 1×10^9, 1×10^{12}

Q6 9.46×10^{12}

Q7 6.9138×10^4

Q8 1.2×10^{-2} (mm)

Q9 a) Mercury
b) Jupiter
c) Mercury
d) Neptune
e) Venus and Mercury
f) Jupiter, Neptune and Saturn

Fractions P.33

Q1 a) $\frac{1}{64}$
b) $\frac{1}{9}$
c) $\frac{1}{18}$
d) $3\frac{29}{32}$
e) $5\frac{5}{32}$
f) $\frac{81}{100\,000}$

Q2 a) 1
b) 4
c) $\frac{1}{2}$
d) $\frac{2}{5}$
e) $\frac{10}{33}$
f) 1000

Q3 a) $\frac{1}{4}$
b) $\frac{5}{6}$
c) $\frac{1}{2}$
d) $4\frac{3}{8}$
e) $5\frac{3}{8}$
f) 1

Q4 $3\frac{7}{15}$, so the bowl will be big enough.

Q5 a) 0
b) $\frac{1}{2}$
c) $-\frac{1}{6}$
d) $1\frac{7}{8}$
e) $-2\frac{7}{8}$
f) $\frac{4}{5}$

Q6 a) $\frac{3}{4}$
b) $\frac{5}{12}$
c) $\frac{7}{15}$
d) $4\frac{3}{4}$
e) 4
f) $1\frac{1}{5}$
g) $\frac{5}{8}$
h) $-\frac{1}{24}$
i) $4\frac{3}{5}$
j) $1\frac{1}{30}$
k) 1
l) $\frac{44}{75}$

Answers: P.34 — P.38

Fractions, Decimals and Percentages P.34

Q1
a) 25%
b) 50%
c) 75%
d) 10%
e) 41.52%
f) 84.06%
g) 39.62%
h) 28.28%

Q2
a) 0.5
b) 0.12
c) 0.4
d) 0.34
e) 0.602
f) 0.549
g) 0.431
h) 0.788

Q3
a) 50%
b) 25%
c) 12.5%
d) 75%
e) 4%
f) 66.7%

Q4
a) 1/4
b) 3/5
c) 9/20
d) 3/10
e) 41/500
f) 62/125
g) 443/500
h) 81/250

Q5 80%

Q6 Grade C

Fractions and Decimals P.35

Q1
a) 0.3   e) 1.75
b) 0.37   f) 0.125
c) 0.4   g) 0.6
d) 0.375   h) 0.05

Q2

Fraction	Decimal
$\frac{1}{2}$	0.5
$\frac{1}{5}$	0.2
$\frac{1}{8}$	0.125
$\frac{8}{5}$	1.6
$\frac{4}{16}$	0.25
$\frac{7}{2}$	3.5
$\frac{x}{10}$	0.x
$\frac{x}{100}$	0.0x
$\frac{3}{20}$	0.15
$\frac{9}{20}$	0.45

Q3
a) $\frac{3}{5}$ e) $\frac{1}{3}$
b) $\frac{3}{4}$ f) $\frac{2}{3}$
c) $\frac{19}{20}$ g) $\frac{1}{9}$
d) $\frac{16}{125}$

Q4
a) $\frac{2}{9}$ e) $\frac{4}{33}$
b) $\frac{4}{9}$ f) $\frac{545}{999}$
c) $\frac{8}{9}$ g) $\frac{753}{999}$ or $\frac{251}{333}$
d) $\frac{80}{99}$ h) $\frac{156}{999}$ or $\frac{52}{333}$

Manipulating Surds and Rational Numbers P.36

Q1
a) e.g. $x = 2$
b) e.g. $x = 4$

Q2
a) irrational
b) rational
c) irrational
d) rational

Q3
a) $\sqrt{2} \times \sqrt{8}$, $(\sqrt{5})^6$, 0.4, $49^{-\frac{1}{2}}$
b) 6π, $\sqrt{6}+6$

Q4
a) rational
b) irrational
c) irrational

Q5
a) $\sqrt{15}$ e) x
b) 2   f) x
c) 1   g) 8
d) 2½   h) $3\left[\sqrt{2} - 1\right]$

Q6 E.g. $x = \sqrt{18}$, $y = \sqrt{2}$ gives
$\frac{x}{y} = \sqrt{9} = 3$.

Q7
a) e.g. 1.5
b) e.g. $\sqrt{2}$, $\sqrt{3}$
c) As P is rational, let $P = \frac{a}{b}$ where a and b are integers. $\frac{1}{P} = \frac{b}{a}$ which is rational.

X and Y Coordinates P.37-P.38

Q1

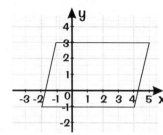

missing coordinate = (5,3)

Q2

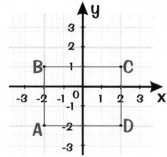

a) B is (1, -3)
b) C is (5, 5)
c) A is (-5, -8)
d) D is (-4, 6)
e) D is (0, -12)
f) C is (-3, 12)

Q3

C = (2, 1), D = (2, -2)

Q4
a) (3,4)
b) (5.5,5)
c) (5.5,11)
d) (8.5,9)
e) (3,3.5)
f) (9.5,9.5)
g) (20,41.5)
h) (30.5,20.5)

Q5 (110, 135)

Q6
a) (2,5.5)
b) (0.5,1.5)
c) (2,–2.5)
d) (1,–1)
e) (2,3)
f) (4,–0.5)
g) (–13,–12.5)
h) (–5,–7)

Answers: *P.39 — P.42*

Straight Line Graphs P.39-P.40

Q1 a) B   f) F
b) A   g) C
c) F   h) B
d) G   i) D
e) E   j) H

Q2

x	-4	-3	-2	-1	0	1	2	3	4
3x	-12	-9	-6	-3	0	3	6	9	12
-1	-1	-1	-1	-1	-1	-1	-1	-1	-1
y	-13	-10	-7	-4	-1	2	5	8	11

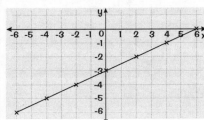

Q3

x	-6	-4	-2	0	2	4	6
½ x	-3	-2	-1	0	1	2	3
-3	-3	-3	-3	-3	-3	-3	-3
y	-6	-5	-4	-3	-2	-1	0

Q4

X	0	3	8
Y	3	9	19

a) 13   c) 4
b) 7   d) 7

Q5

X	-8	-4	8
Y	-5	-4	-1

a) -2.5   c) 4
b) -3   d) 6

Q6

Number of Units used	0	100	200	300
Cost using method A	10	35	60	85
Cost using method B	40	45	50	55

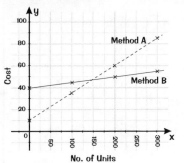

No. of Units

a) i) £27.50   ii) £43.50
b) Method A
c) 150 units

y = mx + c P.41-P.42

Q1 a) $m = 4, (0, 3)$
b) $m = 3, (0, -2)$
c) $m = 2, (0, 1)$
d) $m = -3, (0, 3)$
e) $m = 5, (0, 0)$
f) $m = -2, (0, 3)$
g) $m = -6, (0, -4)$
h) $m = 1, (0, 0)$
i) $m = -\frac{1}{2}, (0, 3)$
j) $m = \frac{1}{4}, (0, 2)$
k) $m = \frac{4}{3}, (0, 2)$
l) $m = -\frac{5}{2}, (0, -2)$
m) $m = \frac{1}{2}, (0, -\frac{3}{2})$
n) $m = \frac{7}{3}, (0, \frac{5}{3})$
o) $m = -1, (0, 0)$
p) $m = 1, (0, 0)$
q) $m = 1, (0, 3)$
r) $m = 1, (0, -3)$
s) $m = 3, (0, 7)$
t) $m = 5, (0, 3)$
u) $m = -2, (0, -3)$
v) $m = 2, (0, 4)$

Q2 a) $-\frac{1}{2}$ g) 4
b) 3   h) 1
c) $-\frac{1}{4}$ i) -1
d) -2   j) $\frac{1}{3}$
e) $-\frac{2}{3}$ k) $-\frac{1}{2}$
f) $-\frac{8}{3}$ l) 3

Q3 a) 2   d) -2
b) $\frac{1}{2}$ e) $\frac{1}{2}$
c) -1   f) $-\frac{3}{4}$

Q4 The gradient is -0.23 so it's a red run.

Q5 a) $y = \frac{7}{2}x - 1$ d) $y = \frac{1}{4}x - 3$
b) $y = \frac{1}{2}x + 4$ e) $y = -\frac{1}{2}x$
c) $y = -\frac{1}{5}x + 7$ f) $y = -2x - 6$

Q6 a) $y = x + 4$ d) $y = -x$
b) $y = 3x + 2$ e) $y = -3x + 4$
c) $y = 2x + 9$ f) $y = -2x - 3$

Q7 a) $y = x$ d) $y = -3x + 3$
b) $y = 3x$ e) $y = -2x - 4$
c) $y = 2x + 1$ f) $y = 5x + 3$

Q8 a) $x = 4$ c) $y = 7$
b) $x = 8$ d) $y = 9$

Q9 (7, 20) and (5, 14)

Answers: P.43 — P.47

Equations from Graphs P.43

Q1

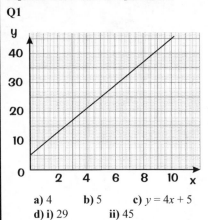

a) 4   **b)** 5   **c)** $y = 4x + 5$
d) i) 29   **ii)** 45

Q2

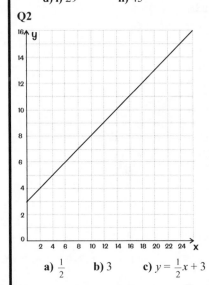

a) $\frac{1}{2}$ **b)** 3   **c)** $y = \frac{1}{2}x + 3$

Q3   a) and **d)**

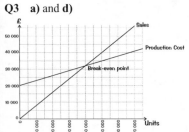

b) Design cost is £20 000.
Manufacturing cost per unit is 30p.
c) $P = 0.3u + 20\,000$ (P = production cost, u = number of units)
e) Break-even point is 40 000 units.

Graphs to Recognise P.44-P.45

Q1 **a)** — xviii)   **l)** — xvii)
b) — x)   **m)** — xiv)
c) — ix)   **n)** — xxi)
d) — iv)   **o)** — viii)
e) — ii)   **p)** — xvi)
f) — xv)   **q)** — vi)
g) — xiii)   **r)** — xix)
h) — xi)   **s)** — v)
i) — i)   **t)** — iii)
j) — vii)   **u)** — xii)
k) — xx)

Quadratic Graphs P.46

Q1

x	-4	-3	-2	-1	0	1	2	3	4
$y=2x^2$	32	18	8	2	0	2	8	18	32

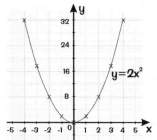

Q2

x	-4	-3	-2	-1	0	1	2	3	4
x^2	16	9	4	1	0	1	4	9	16
$y=x^2+x$	12	6	2	0	0	2	6	12	20

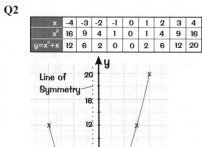

Q3   a)

x	-4	-3	-2	-1	0	1	2	3	4
3	3	3	3	3	3	3	3	3	3
$-x^2$	-16	-9	-4	-1	-0	-1	-4	-9	-16
$y=3-x^2$	-13	-6	-1	2	3	2	-1	-6	-13

b)

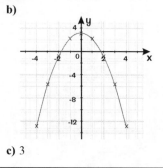

c) 3

Cubic Graphs P.47

Q1

x	-3	-2	-1	0	1	2	3
$y=x^3$	-27	-8	-1	0	1	8	27

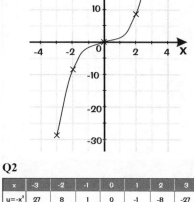

Q2

x	-3	-2	-1	0	1	2	3
$y=-x^3$	27	8	1	0	-1	-8	-27

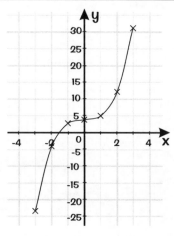

Q3

x	-3	-2	-1	0	1	2	3
x^3	-27	-8	-1	0	1	8	27
+4	4	4	4	4	4	4	4
y	-23	-4	3	4	5	12	31

Answers: P.48 — P.49

Q4

x	-3	-2	-1	0	1	2	3
$-x^3$	27	8	1	0	-1	-8	-27
-4	-4	-4	-4	-4	-4	-4	-4
y	23	4	-3	-4	-5	-12	-31

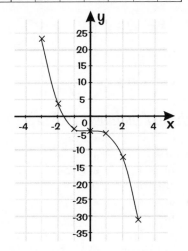

Q5 The graph has been moved 4 units up the *y*-axis.

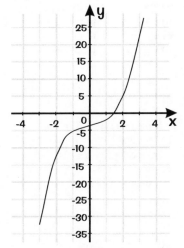

Q6 The graph has been moved 4 units down the *y*-axis.

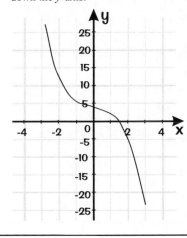

Graphs: Shifts and Stretches
P.48-P.49

Q1 **a)** to **d)**

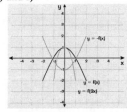

e) and **f)**

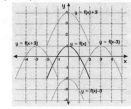

g) and **h)**

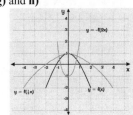

Q2 **a)** to **d)**

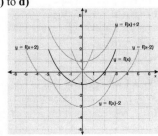

e) and **f)**

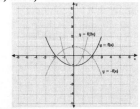

g) to **i)**

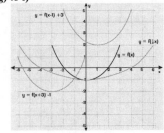

Q3 **a)** and **b)**

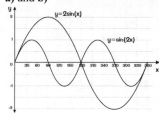

Q4 **a)** and **b)**

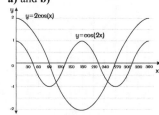

Q5 **a)** to **d)**

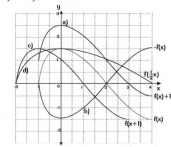

e) to **g)**

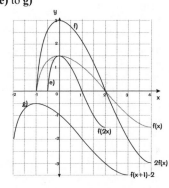

Answers: P.50 — P.55

Algebra P.50-P.51

Q1   **a)** -27°C   **d)** +18°C
      b) -22°C   **e)** +15°C
      c) +12°C   **f)** -12°C

Q2   Expression **b)** is larger by 1.

Q3   **a)** $-4x$ **b)** $18y$

Q4   **a)** $-1000, -10$ **c)** $144, 16$
      b) $-96, -6$ **d)** $0, 0$

Q5   -4

Q6   **a)** $-6xy$ **g)** $\frac{-5x}{y}$
      b) $-16ab$ **h)** 3
      c) $8x^2$ **i)** -4
      d) $-16p^2$ **j)** -10
      e) $\frac{10x}{y}$ **k)** $4x$
      f) $\frac{-10x}{y}$ **l)** $-8y$

Q7   **a)** $15x^2 - x$
      b) $13x^2 - 5x$
      c) $-7x^2 + 12x + 12$
      d) $30abc + 12ab + 4b$
      e) $18pq + 8p$
      f) $17ab - 17a + b$
      g) $4pq - 5p - 9q$
      h) $16x^2 - 4y^2$
      i) $abc + 10ab - 11cd$
      j) $-2x^2 + y^2 - z^2 + 6xy$

Q8   **a)** $4x + 4y - 4z$
      b) $x^2 + 5x$
      c) $-3x + 6$
      d) $9a + 9b$
      e) $-a + 4b$
      f) $2x - 6$
      g) $4e^2 - 2f^2 + 10ef$
      h) $16m - 8n$
      i) $6x^2 + 2x$
      j) $-2ab + 11$
      k) $-2x^2 - xz - 2yz$
      l) $3x - 6y - 5$
      m) $-3a - 4b$
      n) $14pqr + 8pq + 35qr$
      o) $x^3 + x^2$
      p) $4x^3 + 8x^2 + 4x$
      q) $8a^2b + 24ab + 8ab^2$
      r) $7p^2q + 7pq^2 - 7q$
      s) $16x - 8y$

Q9   **a)** $x^2 + 4x + 3x + 12 = x^2 + 7x + 12$
      b) $4x^2 + 6x + 6x + 9 = 4x^2 + 12x + 9$
      c) $15x^2 + 3x + 10x + 2$
          $= 15x^2 + 13x + 2$

Q10 **a)** $x^2 - 2x - 3$
      b) $x^2 + 2x - 15$
      c) $x^2 + 13x + 30$
      d) $x^2 - 7x + 10$
      e) $x^2 - 5x - 14$
      f) $28 - 11x + x^2$
      g) $6x - 2 + 9x^2 - 3x = 9x^2 + 3x - 2$
      h) $6x^2 - 12x + 4x - 8 = 6x^2 - 8x - 8$
      i) $4x^2 + x - 12x - 3 = 4x^2 - 11x - 3$

j) $4x^2 - 8xy + 2xy - 4y^2$
    $= 4x^2 - 4y^2 - 6xy$
k) $12x^2 - 8xy + 24xy - 16y^2$
    $= 12x^2 - 16y^2 + 16xy$
l) $9x^2 + 4y^2 + 12xy$

Q11 $15x^2 + 10x - 6x - 4 = 15x^2 + 4x - 4$

Q12 $4x^2 - 4x + 1$

Q13 **a)** $(4x + 6)$ m
      b) $(-3x^2 + 17x - 10)$ m^2

Q14 **a)** $(8x + 20)$ cm
      b) $40x$ cm^2
      c) $40x - 12x = 28x$ cm^2

Q15 **a)** Perimeter — $3x + 29$ cm
           Area — $\frac{7x + 126}{2}$ cm^2
      b) Perimeter — $(8x + 4)$ cm
           Area — $(3x^2 + 14x - 24)$ cm^2
      c) Perimeter — $(16x - 4)$ cm
           Area — $(16x^2 - 8x + 1)$ cm^2
      d) Perimeter — $(10x + 4)$ cm
           Area — $(6x^2 - 5x - 6)$ cm^2

Q16 **a)** $a^2(b + c)$
      b) $a^2(5 + 13b)$
      c) $a^2(2b + 3c)$
      d) $a^2(a + y)$
      e) $a^2(2x + 3y + 4z)$
      f) $a^2(b^2 + ac^2)$

Q17 **a)** $4xyz(1 + 2) = 12xyz$
      b) $4xyz(2 + 3) = 20xyz$
      c) $8xyz(1 + 2x)$
      d) $4xyz^2(5xy + 4)$

Sequences P.52-P.53

Q1   **a)** 9, 11, 13, add 2 each time
      b) 32, 64, 128, multiply by 2 each time
      c) 30000, 300000, 3000000, multiply by 10 each time
      d) 19, 23, 27, add 4 each time
      e) -6, -11, -16, take 5 off each time

Q2   **a)** 4, 7, 10, 13, 16
      b) 3, 8, 13, 18, 23
      c) 1, 4, 9, 16, 25
      d) -2, 1, 6, 13, 22

Q3   **a)** $2n$
      b) $2n - 1$
      c) $5n$
      d) $3n + 2$

Q4   **a)** 19, 22, 25, $3n + 4$
      b) 32, 37, 42, $5n + 7$
      c) 46, 56, 66, $10n - 4$
      d) 82, 89, 96, $7n + 47$

Q5   **a)** $16\frac{7}{8}, 16\frac{9}{16}, 16\frac{23}{32}, 16\frac{41}{64}$
      b) The 10th term will be the mean of the 8th and 9th.

Q6   **a)** The groups have 3, 8 and 15 triangles.
      b) 24, 35, 48
      c) $(n + 1)^2 - 1$ or $n^2 + 2n$

Q7   **a)** 23, 30, 38, $\frac{1}{2}(n^2 + 3n + 6)$
      b) 30, 41, 54, $n^2 + 5$
      c) 45, 64, 87, $2n^2 - 3n + 10$
      d) 52, 69, 89, $\frac{1}{2}(3n^2 + n + 24)$

Q8   **a)** $\frac{(2n + 1)^2 + 1}{2}$
      b) $\frac{(2n + 1)^2 - 1}{2}$
      c) $(2n + 1)^2$

Solving Equations P.54-P.55

Q1   1

Q2   **a)** $x = 5$ **d)** $x = -6$
      b) $x = 4$ **e)** $x = 5$
      c) $x = 10$ **f)** $x = 9$

Q3   **a)** $x = 5$ **d)** $x = 17$
      b) $x = 2$ **e)** $x = 6$
      c) $x = 8$ **f)** $x = 5$

Q4   **a)** 15.5 cm   **b)** 37.2 cm

Q5   £15.50

Q6   **a)** $x = 9$ **g)** $x = 15$
      b) $x = 2$ **h)** $x = 110$
      c) $x = 3$ **i)** $x = 7\frac{1}{2}$
      d) $x = 3$ **j)** $x = 66$
      e) $x = 4$ **k)** $x = 700$
      f) $x = -1$

Q7   **a)** Joan — £x
           Kate — £$2x$
           Linda — £$(x - 232)$
      b) $4x = 2632$
           $x = 658$
      c) Kate — £1316
           Linda — £426

Q8   **a)** $2x + 32$ cm
      b) $12x$ cm^2
      c) $x = 3.2$

Q9   **a)** $x = 0.75$ **d)** $x = -1$
      b) $x = -1$ **e)** $x = 4$
      c) $x = -6$ **f)** $x = 13$

Q10 $x = 8$

Q11 $x = 1$

Q12 8 yrs

Q13 39, 35, 8

Q14 **a)** $y = 22$ **d)** $x = 19$
      b) $x = 8$ **e)** $x = 23$
      c) $x = 7$ **f)** $z = -5$

Q15 $x = 1\frac{1}{2}$

Q16 **a)** $x = 5$ **b)** $x = 9$

Q17 $x = 1\frac{1}{2}$ AB = 5 cm
                 AC = 5½ cm
                 BC = 7½ cm

Answers: P.56 — P.60

Rearranging Formulas P.56-P.57

Q1 **a)** $h = \dfrac{10 - g}{4}$

b) $c = 2d - 4$

c) $k = 3 + \dfrac{j}{2}$

d) $b = \dfrac{3a}{2}$

e) $g = \dfrac{8f}{3}$

f) $x = 2(y + 3)$

g) $t = 6(s - 10)$

Q2 **a)** $c = \dfrac{w - 500m}{50}$

b) 132

Q3 **a) i)** £38.00   **ii)** £48.00
b) $c = 28 + 0.25n$
c) $n = 4(c - 28)$
d) i) 24 miles **ii)** 88 miles
   iii) 114 miles

Q4 **a)** $x = y^2 - 3$

b) $g = \dfrac{4\pi^2 l}{t^2}$

c) $g = 3f - 10$

d) $z = 5 - 2w$

Q5 **a)** £Jx

b) $P = T - Jx$

c) $J = \dfrac{T - P}{x}$

d) £16

Q6 **a) i)** £2.04   **ii)** £3.48
b) $C = (12x + 60)$ pence

c) $x = \dfrac{C - 60}{12}$

d) i) 36   **ii)** 48   **iii)** 96

Q7 **a)** $x = \dfrac{z}{y + 2}$

b) $x = \dfrac{b}{a - 3}$

c) $x = \dfrac{y}{4 - z}$

d) $x = \dfrac{3z + y}{y + 5}$

e) $x = \dfrac{-2}{y - z}$ or $\dfrac{2}{z - y}$

f) $x = \dfrac{2y + 3z}{2 - z}$

g) $x = \dfrac{-y - wz}{yz - 1}$ or $\dfrac{y + wz}{1 - yz}$

h) $x = \dfrac{-z}{4}$

Q8 **a)** $p = \dfrac{4r - 2q}{q - 3}$

b) $g = \dfrac{5 - 2e}{f + 2}$

c) $b = \dfrac{3c + 2a}{a - c}$

d) $a = \dfrac{2c + 4b}{4 + c - d}$

e) $x = \left(\dfrac{4 - y}{2 - z}\right)^2$

f) $a = \dfrac{b^2}{3 + b}$

g) $m = -7n$

h) $e = \dfrac{d}{50}$

i) $y = \dfrac{x}{3x + 2}$

Q9 **a)** $y = \dfrac{x}{x - 1}$

b) $y = \dfrac{-3 - 2x}{x - 1}$ or $\dfrac{2x + 3}{1 - x}$

Inequalities P.58-P.59

Q1 **a)** $9 \le x < 13$
b) $-4 \le x < 1$
c) $x \ge -4$
d) $x < 5$
e) $x > 25$
f) $-1 < x \le 3$
g) $0 < x \le 5$
h) $x < -2$

Q2

a)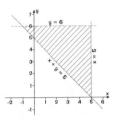

Q3 **a)** $x > 3$
b) $x < 4$
c) $x \le 5$
d) $x \le 6$
e) $x \ge 7.5$
f) $x < 4$
g) $x < 7$
h) $x < 4$
i) $x \ge 3$
j) $x > 11$
k) $x < 3$
l) $x \ge -\frac{1}{2}$
m) $x \le -2$
n) $x > 5$
o) $x < 15$
p) $x \ge -2$

Q4 Largest integer for x is 2.

Q5 $\dfrac{11 - x}{2} < 5, \; x > 1$

Q6 $1130 \le 32x$
36 classrooms are needed.

Q7 50 guests (including bride and groom), $900 \ge 18x$

Q8 $x \ge 2, \quad y > 1, \quad 5 \ge x + y$

Q9

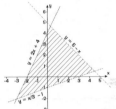

Q10

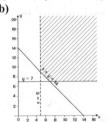

Q11 **a)** $x > 5, \quad y \ge 7, \quad x + y \ge 14$
b)

Simultaneous Equations and Graphs P.60

Q1 **a)** $x = 3, y = 3$
b) $x = 2, y = 5$
c) $x = 1, y = 2$
d) $x = 1, y = 2$
e) $x = 1, y = 4$
f) $x = 1, y = 2$
g) $x = 2, y = 3$
h) $x = 2, y = 3$
i) $x = 5, y = 2$
j) $x = 3, y = 4$

Q2 **a)** $x = -2$
b) $x = 0.5$
c) $x = 0.5$
d) $x = 3$

Answers: P.61 — P.67

Simultaneous Equations P.61

Q1 **a)** $x = 1, y = 2$
b) $x = 0, y = 3$
c) $x = -1\frac{1}{2}, y = 4$

Q2 **a)** $6x + 5y = 430$
$4x + 10y = 500$
b) $x = 45, y = 32$

Q3 7 chickens
4 cats

Q4 5 g (jellies are 4 g)

Q5 $3y + 2x = 18$
$y + 3x = 6$ $x = 0, y = 6$

$4y + 5x = 7$
$2x - 3y = 12$ $x = 3, y = -2$

$4x - 6y = 13$
$x + y = 2$ $x = 2\frac{1}{2}, y = -\frac{1}{2}$

Q6 $5m + 2c = 344$
$4m + 3c = 397$
$m = 34p, c = 87p$

Q7 $x = 12, y = 2$

Symmetry P.62-P.63

Q1

a) **b)** **c)**

d) **e)** **f)**

Q2 **a)** 6   **b)** 8
c) 5   **d)** 3

Q3

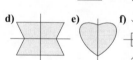

M   H   V   B
1   2   1   1

Order of Rotation
1   1   2

A   K   Z

Q4 No

Q5 Four. Three like this:

and one through its middle:

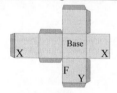

Q6 Infinitely many.

Q7 No

Q8

One of the following:

Q9 A point

Q10 **a)** Two, one longitudinal and one perpendicular to that.
b) 90°
c) They meet in a line.

Q11 **a)** 4
b) Yes it is true.

The Shapes you Need to Know P.64

Q1 Missing words (reading down):
Rectangle, parallelogram, parallel, two, equal

Missing drawings:

Q2 **a)** 2, 2
b) equilateral
c) no, no
d) right-angled

Shapes and Angles P.65

Q1 **a)** acute, 43°
b) obtuse, 143°
c) right, 90°
d) reflex, 301°
e) reflex, 248°
f) acute, 16°

Q2 Parallelograms have two pairs of equal angles, so one of the missing angles will be 52°.
Sum of interior angles = 360°
So two interior angles
= 360° − (2 × 52°) = 256°
256° ÷ 2 = 128°
So the three other angles will be 52°, 128° and 128°.

Nets and Projections P.66-P.67

Q1

Other arrangements are possible.

Q2

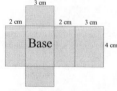

Other arrangements are possible.

Q3

Q4 **a)** Rectangle.
b) AH, CF, BG.
c) DF, AG, BH.
d) HC, BE, AF.
e) 8

Q5 **a)** 1
b) 1

Q6 **a)** H, F and D
b) Line symmetry through lines AF, DH, BG and CE. Rotational symmetry of order 4.
c) 5 faces and vertices, 8 edges.

Q7 **a)** I
b) 64 cm²
c) 64 × 6 = 384 cm²
d)

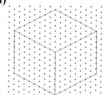

Q8 E.g.

Q9 Net B

Q10 **a)** Front elevation:

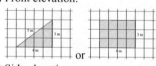

or

b) Side elevation:

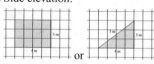

or

c) Plan:

Answers: P.68 — P.73

Geometry P.68-P.69

Q1 a) $x = 47°$
b) $y = 154°$
c) $z = 22°$
d) $p = 35°$, $q = 45°$

Q2 a) $a = 146°$
b) $m = 131°$, $z = 48°$
c) $x = 68°$, $p = 112°$
d) $s = 20°$, $t = 90°$

Q3 a) $x = 96°$, $p = 38°$
b) $a = 108°$, $b = 23°$, $c = 95°$
c) $d = 120°$, $e = 60°$, $f = 60°$, $g = 120°$
d) $h = 155°$, $i = 77.5°$, $j = 102.5°$,
$k = 77.5°$

Q4 a) $b = 70°$ $c = 30°$
$d = 50°$ $e = 60°$
$f = 150°$
b) $g = 21°$ $h = 71°$
$i = 80°$ $j = 38°$
$k = 92°$
c) $l = 35°$ $m = 145°$
$n = 55°$ $p = 125°$

Q5 a) $x = 162°$ $y = 18°$
b) $x = 87°$ $y = 93°$
$z = 93°$
c) $a = 30°$ $2a = 60°$
$5a = 150°$ $4a = 120°$

Q6 a) $a = 141°$, $b = 141°$, $c = 39°$,
$d = 141°$, $e = 39°$
b) $a = 47°$, $b = 47°$, $c = 133°$, $d = 43°$
$e = 43°$
c) $m = 140°$, $n = 140°$, $p = 134°$,
$q = 46°$, $r = 40°$

Circle Geometry P.70-P.71

Q1 a) BAD = 80° (opposite angle C in cyclic quadrilateral)
b) EAB = 180 – 80 – 30 = 70°

Q2 a) BD = 5 cm (as the tangents BD and CD are equal).
b) Angle COD = 70° (= 180° – (20° + 90°)), since the tangent CD meets the radius OC at an angle of 90°.
c) Angle COB = 140° (since angle BOD equals angle COD).
d) Angle CAB = 70° (since the angle at the centre (COB) is twice the angle at the edge (CAB)).

Q3 a) BOE = 106° (angle at centre)
b) ACE = 32° (angle in opposite segment)

Q4 a) ACD = 70° (angle in opposite segment)
b) BAD = 180 – (30 + 70) = 80° (opposite angles of a cyclic quadrilateral total 180°)

Q5 a) Angles in the same segment.
b) $3x + 40 = 6x – 50$
$90 = 3x$
$30 = x$
angle ABD = 3(30) + 40 = 130°

Q6 a) Angle ABD = 70° (angle at centre = 2 × angle at circumference)
b) Angle ABC = 90° (angle in semicircle)
c) Angle DBC = 20° (90° – 70°)

Q7 a) 90° (angle in a semicircle)
b) The angle at A = 90° (tangent and radius are perpendicular). The third angle in the triangle is 180 – 90 – 23 = 67° and so $x = 90 – 67 = 23°$.
Or, by opposite segment theorem:
x = angle ABC = 23°.

Q8 a) With AD as a chord, angle ABD = ACD = 30° (same segment); angle AXB = 85° (vertically opposite angles). The third angles must be the same in both triangles so the triangles must be similar.
b) Ratio of lengths $= \frac{4}{8} = \frac{1}{2}$
so XB = 5 cm
c) angle BDC = 180 – 85 – 30 = 65°

Q9 90° (angle in a semicircle)

The Four Transformations P.72-P.73

Q1 a) to e) — see diagram.

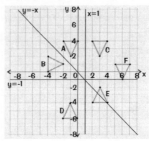

f) Rotation of 180°, centre (3, 0)

Q2 a), b), d), e) — see diagram

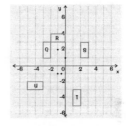

c) Rotation 180° about (0, 2).
f) 90° rotation anticlockwise about $\left(-\frac{1}{2}, -\frac{1}{2}\right)$.

Q3 a), b) — see diagram.

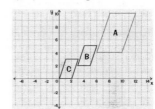

c) Ratio of areas C:A = 1:4

Q4 a), b), c) — see diagram.

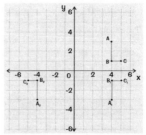

d) Rotation of 180° about (0, 0)

Answers: P.74 — P.77

Enlargement P.74

Q1 **a)** PT = 4.5m
b) Ratio of lengths = 1.5:4.5 = 1:3
So ST = 3 × QR = 3 × 0.9 = 2.7 m

Q2 **a)** 1250 ÷ 500 = 2.5
b) 800 pixels

Q3 **a)** Ratio AC:AQ = 24:7.5 = 3.2:1 so
AP = 15 × $\frac{1}{3.2}$ = 4.6875 cm
b) Using ½(base)(height) = ½(24)(9)
= 108 cm²
c) Sides scale factor = $\frac{1}{3.2}$
Area scale factor = $\frac{1}{10.24}$
Area of triangle APQ = 108 × $\frac{1}{10.24}$
= 10.5 cm²

Probability P.75-P.77

Q1 **a)** 1/2
b) 2/3
c) 1/6
d) 0

And so should be arranged
<u>approximately</u> like this on the
number line.

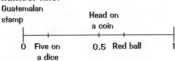

Q2 Debbie's chance of winning would be
1/9. This is greater than 0.1, so she
would choose to play.

Q3 The probability of a head is still 1/2

Q4 1 – 0.27 = 0.73 or 73/100

Q5 **a)** 5/12
b) 4/12 = 1/3
c) 3/12 = 1/4
d) 9/12 = 3/4

Q6 **a)** 40/132 = 10/33
b) P(car being blue or green) = 45/132
P(not blue or green) = 87/132
= 29/44

Q7 **a)** 1/4
b) 1/4 × 100 = approx 25 days

Q8 **a)**

Outcome	Frequency
W	8
D	5
L	7

b) The 3 outcomes are not equally
likely.
c) 1/4
d) They are most likely to win.

Q9 **a)** $\frac{1}{13}$
b) $\frac{2}{39}$ **c)** $\frac{1}{36}$

Q10 **a)** $\frac{7}{12}$ **b)** $\frac{7}{12}$
c) The two are not mutually
exclusive (or other equivalent
answer).

Q11 **a)** $\frac{2}{5}$
b) $\frac{4}{15}$ **c)** $\frac{2}{3}$

Q12 **a)**

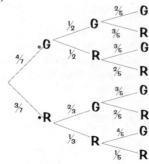

b) $\frac{18}{35}$
c) $\frac{3}{7}$

Q13 4 times

Q14 **a)**

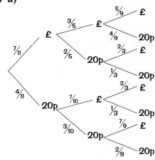

b) $\frac{28}{55}$ **c)** $\frac{46}{165}$

Q15 $\frac{1}{28}$

Answers: P.78 — P.83

Unit 3

Ratios P.78-P.79

Q1 **a)** 3:4   **d)** 9:16
    b) 1:4   **e)** 7:2
    c) 1:2   **f)** 9:1

Q2 **a)** 6 cm   **d)** 1.5 cm
    b) 11 cm   **e)** 2.75 cm
    c) 30.4 m   **f)** 7.6 m

Q3 **a)** £8, £12
    b) 80 m, 70 m
    c) 100 g, 200 g, 200 g.
    d) 1hr 20 m, 2 hr 40 m, 4 hrs.

Q4 **a)** £4.80
    b) 80 cm

Q5 John 4, Peter 12

Q6 400 ml, 600 ml, 1000 ml

Q7 30

Q8 Jane £40, Holly £48, Rosemary £12

Q9 Paul — £16

Q10 **a)** 250/500 = 1/2
    b) 150/500 = 3/10

Q11 **a)** 245 girls   **b)** 210 boys

Q12 **a)** £39
    b) £140

Q13 **a)** 1:300
    b) 6 m
    c) 3.3 cm

Q14 **a)** 15 kg
    b) 30 kg
    c) 8 kg cement, 24 kg sand and 48 kg gravel.

Q15 **a)** 30 fine
    b) 15 not fine
    c) 30/45 = 2/3

Q16 **a)** 45 Salt & Vinegar
    b) 90 bags sold altogether

Travel Graphs P.80-P.81

Q1 **a)** 4 km
    b) 15 mins and 45 mins
    c) 2.4 km/h
    d) 1100
    e) 10 km/h
    f) 1030

Q2 **a)** 85 mins
    b) 80 mins
    c) 16.9 mph
    d) 57.6 mph
    e) No, because the total driving time is 80 minutes.

Q3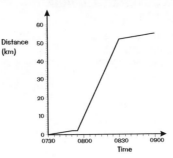

He waited for 5 mins.

Q4 **a)** A 80.0 km/h, fastest.
     B 57.1 km/h
     C 66.7 km/h
     D 44.4 km/h
     E 50.0 km/h
    b) steepest slope was fastest, least steep slope was slowest.

Q5 **a)** B
    b) 3¾ mins
    c) B
    d) i) 267 m/min   **ii)** 16.0 km/h
    e) C was the fastest; 700 m/min or 42 km/h

Q6 **a)**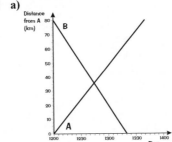
    b) accept 1243-1245
    c) accept 35-36 km

Q7 **a)**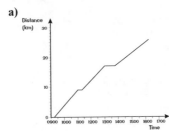
    b) 25.75 km
    c) 3.68 km/h
    d) Her fastest speed was in the first section (steepest graph) — her speed was 5.14 km/h.

Areas and Gradients of Graphs P.82

Q1 **a) i)** 90 km
     ii) 150 km
    b) 320 km

Q2 **a) i)** 17.5 km
     ii) 50 km
    b) 102.5 km

Q3 **a)** 140 m
    b) 10 m/s^2

Q4 **a)** Approximately 117 m
    b) Approximately 5-6 m/s^2

Direct and Inverse Proportion P.83

Q1 £247.80

Q2 112 hours

Q3 **a)** $9\frac{1}{3}$ cm
    b) 30.45 km

Q4 $y = 20$

Q5

x	2	4	6
y	5	10	15

x	3	6	9
y	4.5	9	13.5

x	27	54	81
y	5	10	15

Q6 $x = 2$

Q7

x	1	2	3	4	5	6
y	48	24	16	12	9.6	8

Q8 4 kg

Answers: P.84 — P.88

Factorising Quadratics P.84

Q1 **a)** $(x + 5)(x - 2)$
  $x = -5, x = 2$
  b) $(x - 3)(x - 2)$
  $x = 3, x = 2$
  c) $(x - 1)^2$
  $x = 1$
  d) $(x - 3)(x - 1)$
  $x = 3, x = 1$
  e) $(x - 5)(x + 4)$
  $x = 5, x = -4$
  f) $(x + 1)(x - 5)$
  $x = -1, x = 5$
  g) $(x + 7)(x - 1)$
  $x = -7, x = 1$
  h) $(x + 7)^2$
  $x = -7$
  i) $(x - 5)(x + 3)$
  $x = 5, x = -3$

Q2 **a)** $(x + 8)(x - 2)$
  $x = -8, x = 2$
  b) $(x + 9)(x - 4)$
  $x = -9, x = 4$
  c) $(x + 9)(x - 5)$
  $x = -9, x = 5$
  d) $x(x - 5)$
  $x = 0, x = 5$
  e) $x(x - 11)$
  $x = 0, x = 11$
  f) $(x - 7)(x + 3)$
  $x = 7, x = -3$
  g) $(x - 30)(x + 10)$
  $x = 30, x = -10$
  h) $(x - 24)(x - 2)$
  $x = 24, x = 2$
  i) $(x - 9)(x - 4)$
  $x = 9, x = 4$
  j) $(x + 7)(x - 2)$
  $x = -7, x = 2$
  k) $(x + 7)(x - 3)$
  $x = -7, x = 3$
  l) $(x - 5)(x + 2)$
  $x = 5, x = -2$
  m) $(x - 6)(x + 3)$
  $x = 6, x = -3$
  n) $(x - 9)(x + 7)$
  $x = 9, x = -7$
  o) $(x + 4)(x - 3)$
  $x = -4, x = 3$

Q3 $x = \frac{1}{2}, x = -\frac{1}{2}$

Q4 $x = 4$

Q5 **a)** $(x^2 - x)$ m^2
  b) $x = 3$

Q6 **a)** $x(x + 1)$ cm^2
  b) $x = 3$

Q7 **a)** x^2 m^2
  b) $12x$ m^2
  c) $x^2 + 12x - 64 = 0$
  $x = 4$

The Quadratic Formula P.85-P.86

Q1 **a)** 1.87, 0.13
  b) 2.39, 0.28
  c) 1.60, - 3.60
  d) 1.16, -3.16
  e) 0.53, -4.53
  f) -11.92, -15.08
  g) -2.05, -4.62
  h) 0.84, 0.03

Q2 **a)** -2, -6
  b) 0.67, -0.5
  c) 3, -2
  d) 2, 1
  e) 3, 0.75
  f) 3, 0
  g) 0.67
  h) 0, -2.67
  i) 4, -0.5
  j) 4, -5
  k) 1, -3
  l) 5, -1.33
  m) 1.5, -1
  n) -2.5, 1
  o) 0.5, 0.33
  p) 1, -3
  q) 2, -6
  r) 2, -4

Q3 **a)** 0.30, -3.30
  b) 3.65, -1.65
  c) 0.62, -1.62
  d) -0.55, -5.45
  e) -0.44, -4.56
  f) 1.62, -0.62
  g) 0.67, -4.00
  h) -0.59, -3.41
  i) 7.12, -1.12
  j) 13.16, 0.84
  k) 1.19, -4.19
  l) 1.61, 0.53
  m) 0.44, -3.44
  n) 2.78, 0.72

Q4 **a)** 1.70, -4.70
  b) -0.27, -3.73
  c) 1.88, -0.88
  d) 0.12, -4.12
  e) 4.83, -0.83
  f) 1.62, -0.62
  g) 1.12, -1.79
  h) -0.21, -4.79
  i) 2.69, -0.19
  j) 2.78, 0.72
  k) 1, 0
  l) 1.5, 0.50

Q5 $x^2 - 3.6x + 3.24 = 0$
  $x = 1.8$

Q6 **a)** $x^2 + 2.5x - 144.29 = 0$
  $x = 10.83$
  b) 48.3 cm

Quadratic Equations and Graphs P.87

Q1 **a)** $x = 0, x = 1$
  b) $x = 2.7, x = -0.7$
  c) $x = 3.4, x = -2.4$
  d) $x = 1.6, x = -2.6$
  e) $x = 3.4, x = -2.4$
  f) $x = 1.6, x = -2.6$

Q2

x	-4	-3	-2	-1	0	1	2	3	4
$-\frac{1}{2}x^2$	-8	-4.5	-2	-0.5	0	-0.5	-2	-4.5	-8
+5	5	5	5	5	5	5	5	5	5
y	-3	0.5	3	4.5	5	4.5	3	0.5	-3

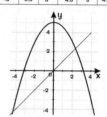

  a) $x = 3.2, x = -3.2$
  b) $x = 4, x = -4$
  c) $x = 2.3, x = -4.3$

Trial and Improvement P.88

Q1

Guess (x)	value of $x^3 + x$	Too large or too small
2	$2^3 + 2 = 10$	Too small
3	$3^3 + 3 = 30$	Too large
2.6	$(2.6)^3 + 2.6 = 20.2$	Too small
2.7	$(2.7)^3 + 2.7 = 22.4$	Too small
2.8	$(2.8)^3 + 2.8 = 24.8$	Too large
2.75	$(2.75)^3 + 2.75 = 23.5$	Too small

∴ To 1 d.p the solution is x=2.8

Q2

Guess (x)	value of $x^3 + x^2 - 4x$	Too large or too small
-3	$(-3)^3 + (-3)^2 - 4(-3) = -6$	Too small
-2	$(-2)^3 + (-2)^2 - 4(-2) = 4$	Too large
-2.1	$(-2.1)^3 + (-2.1)^2 - 4(-2.1) = 3.549$	Too large
-2.2	$(-2.2)^3 + (-2.2)^2 - 4(-2.2) = 2.99$	Too small
-2.15	$(-2.15)^3 + (-2.15)^2 - 4(-2.15) = 3.3$	Too large

∴ To 1 d.p the solution is x=-2.2

Guess (x)	value of $x^3 + x^2 - 4x$	Too large or too small
-1	$-1 + 1 + 4 = 4$	Too large
0	$0 + 0 - 0 = 0$	Too small
-0.8	$(-0.8)^3 + (-0.8)^2 - 4(-0.8) = 3.328$	Too large
-0.7	$(-0.7)^3 + (-0.7)^2 - 4(-0.7) = 2.947$	Too small
-0.75	$(-0.75)^3 + (-0.75)^2 - 4(-0.75) = 3.141$	Too large

∴ To 1 d.p the solution is x=-0.7

Guess (x)	value of $x^3 + x^2 - 4x$	Too large or too small
1	$1 + 1 - 4 = -2$	Too small
2	$8 + 4 - 8 = 4$	Too large
1.9	$(1.9)^3 + (1.9)^2 - 4(1.9) = 2.869$	Too small
1.95	$(1.95)^3 + (1.95)^2 - 4(1.95) = 3.417$	Too large

∴ To 1 d.p the solution is x=1.9

Q3 Try different values of x to 1 d.p. between 3 and 4 to see which gives the highest value of V, e.g:

Guess (x)	value of $4x^3-80x^2+400x$
3	108−720+1200 = 588
4	256−1280+1600 = 576
3.5	171.5−980+1400 = 591.5
3.4	157.216−924.8+1360 = 592.416
3.3	143.748−871.2+1320 = 592.548
3.2	131.072−819.2+1280 = 591.872

∴ To 1 d.p the solution is x=3.3

Polygons P.89

Q1 Isosceles.

Q2 **a)** $90° + 60° = 150°$

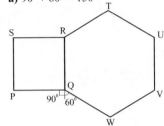

b)

∠PRW = 75°

c) $180 - (360/n) = 150$
$180n - 360 = 150n$
$30n = 360 \Rightarrow n = 12$

Q3 $540° - (100° + 104° + 120°)$
$= 216°$ for two equal angles
∴1 angle $= 108°$

Q4 **a)** Interior angle $= 165°$
b) Exterior angle $= 180° - 165° = 15°$
Sum of exterior angles $= 15 \times 24$
$= 360°$

Q5 **a)** $\frac{360}{5} = 72°$
b) $\frac{180 - 72}{2} = 54°$
c) i) $90°$
ii) $36°$
d) $36°$ (angle in the opposite segment)

Q6 $(n - 2)180 = 2520$, $n = 16$

Similarity P.90

Q1 **a)** Angle A shared. Parallel lines make corresponding angles equal so the triangles are similar.
b) Ratio of lengths given by
$\frac{AB}{AD} = \frac{12}{20} = \frac{3}{5}$
So $x = 25 \times \frac{3}{5} = 15$ cm
Also $\frac{y + 10}{y} = \frac{5}{3}$
$\Rightarrow 2y = 30$, $y = 15$ cm

Q2 **a)** All lengths must be enlarged in the same ratio for them to be similar.
b) 4 litres

Q3 **a)** Triangles APQ and STC (both isosceles and share either angle A or C)
b) Ratio AC:AQ $= 24:7.5 = 3.2:1$ so
AP $= 15 \times \frac{1}{3.2} = 4.6875$ cm
PT $= 24 - 2 (4.6875)$
$= 14.625$ cm.
c) Using $\frac{1}{2}$(base)(height)
$= \frac{1}{2}(24)(9) = 108$ cm²
d) Scale factor $= \frac{1}{3.2}$
Area scale factor $= \frac{1}{10.24}$
Area of triangle APQ $= 108 \times \frac{1}{10.24} = 10.5$ cm²
e) $108 - 2 (10.5) = 87$ cm²

Q4 **a)** volume $= \frac{1}{3}\pi(100^2)(100)$
$= 1047198$ cm³
$= 1.05$ m³
b) 50 cm
c) ratio $= 1:2^3 = 1:8$
d) Volume of small cone $=$
$1.05 \times \frac{1}{8} = 0.131$ m³
e) volume of portion left $=$
$1.05 - 0.131 = 0.919$
so ratio $= 0.919:0.131 = \frac{0.919}{0.131}:1$
$= 7:1$

Pythagoras' Theorem P.91

Q1 **a)** 10.8 cm   **f)** 7.89 m
b) 6.10 m   **g)** 9.60 cm
c) 5 cm   **h)** 4.97 cm
d) 27.0 mm   **i)** 6.80 cm
e) 8.49 m   **j)** 8.5 cm

Q2 a = 3.32 cm   f = 8.62 m
b = 6 cm   g = 6.42 m
c = 6.26 m   h = 19.2 mm
d = 5.6 mm   i = 9.65 m
e = 7.08 mm   j = 48.7 mm

Q3 k = 6.55 cm   q = 7.07 cm
l = 4.87 m   r = 7.50 m
m = 6.01 m   s = 9.45 mm
n = 12.4 m   t = 4.33 cm
p = 5.22 m   u = 7.14 m

Q4 9.7 m

Pythagoras' Theorem and Congruence P.92

Q1 314 m

Q2 **a)** 12 cm, 7.94 cm
b) 40.9 cm
c) 89.7 cm²

Q3 ABC and DEF are congruent — same size angles and side lengths.

Q4

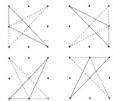

Hence 7 ways to draw another.

Trigonometry P.93-P.94

	(tan)	(sin)	(cos)
Q1 a)	0.306	0.292	0.956
b)	8.14	0.993	0.122
c)	0.0875	0.0872	0.996
d)	0.532	0.469	0.883
e)	1	0.707	0.707

Q2 a = 1.40 cm
b = 6 cm
θ = 28.1°
c = 5.31 cm
d = 10.8 cm

Q3 e = 12.6 cm
f = 11.3 cm
θ = 49.5°
g = 6.71 m
h = 30.1 cm

Q4 i = 4.89 cm
j = 3.79 cm
θ = 52.4°
k = 5.32 cm
l = 41.6 cm

Q5 m = 11.3 cm
n = 18.8 cm
p = 8.62 cm
q = 21.3 cm
r = 54.6°
t = 59.8 cm
u = 14.5 cm
v = 11.7 cm
w = 11.7 cm

Answers: P.95 — P.98

Q6 a)

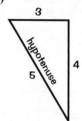

b) 36.9°

Q7 62°

Q8 20.5°

Q9

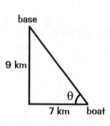

θ = 52.1°, bearing = 322°

Q10

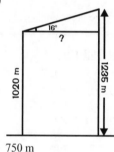

Q11

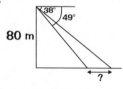

25.8 m

Q12

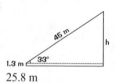

a) 102.4 m, 69.5 m
b) 32.9 m

Q13

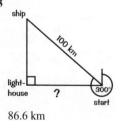

86.6 km

3D Pythagoras and Trigonometry P95

Q1 a) 59.0°
   b) 23.3 cm
   c) 25 cm
   d) 21.1°

Q2 a) 42.5 cm
   b) 50.9 cm

Q3 a) 36.1 cm, 21.5 cm, 31.0 cm
   b) 36.9 cm

Q4 a) 15.4 cm
   b) 20.4 cm

Q5 The 85p box

Q6 a) 3.82 cm
   b) 45.8 cm^2
   c) 137.5 cm^3

The Sine and Cosine Rules P.96-P.97

Q1 $a = 4.80$ cm $f = 5.26$ cm
   $b = 25.8$ mm $g = 9.96$ cm
   $c = 13.0$ cm $h = 20.2$ mm
   $d = 8.89$ m $i = 3.72$ m
   $e = 18.4$ cm $j = 8.29$ cm

Q2 $k = 51°$ $q = 36°$
   $l = 46°$ $r = 64°$
   $m = 43°$ $s = 18°$
   $n = 88°$ $t = 49°$
   $p = 45°$

Q3 $a = 63°$ $f = 68°$
   $b = 45°$ $g = 203$ mm
   $c = 8.9$ cm $h = 127$ mm
   $d = 27°$
   $e = 10.5$ cm

Q4 a) 46°
   b) 52°   **c)** 82°

Q5 12.0 m

Q6

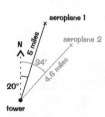

Distance = 1.2 miles.
The alarm should be ringing
because the planes are less than
3 miles apart, so the software seems
reliable.

Q7

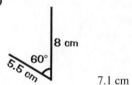

a) 86°
b) 323 km
c) 215°

Q8 a)

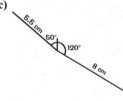

b)

14.5 cm
(118.5° comes from the fact that the
minute hand is at 19.75 mins.
19.75 ÷ 60 × 360 = 118.5.)

c)

13.5 cm

Q9 Height of building = 35 m

The Graphs of Sin, Cos and Tan P.98

Q1 A(180,0)
   B(90,1)   C(−90,−1)

Q2 D(270,0) F(0,1)
   E(90,0)   G(−90,0)

Q3 H(180,0)
   I(−45,−1) J(45,1)

Q4 A $y = \sin(x)$ and $y = \tan(x)$
   B $y = \cos(x)$
   C $y = \cos(x)$
   D $y = \sin(x)$ and $y = \tan(x)$
   E $y = \sin(x)$
   F $y = \tan(x)$
   G $y = \sin(x)$ and $y = \tan(x)$
   H $y = \cos(x)$
   I $y = \sin(x)$
   J $y = \cos(x)$

Answers: P.99 — P.103

Angles of Any Size P.99-P.100

(Answers to Qns.1- 4 are given to the nearest degree.)

Q1 **a)** –510°, –390°, –150°, –30°, 210°, 330°, 570°, 690°.
b) –714°, –546°, –354°, –186°, 6°, 174°, 366°, 534°.
c) –476°, –424°, –116°, –64°, 244°, 296°, 604°, 656°.

Q2 **a)** –694°, –386°, –334°, –26°, 26°, 334°, 386°, 694°.
b) –660°, –420°, –300°, –60°, 60°, 300°, 420°, 660°.
c) –593°, –487°, –233°, –127°, 127°, 233°, 487°, 593°.
Cos graph has the y-axis as a line of symmetry, the sin graph does not.

Q3 **a)** –405°, –225°, –45°, 135°, 315°.
b) –333°, –153°, 27°, 207°, 387°.
c) –288°, –108°, 72°, 252°, 432°.

Q4 **a)** e.g. –337°, –203°, 23°, 157°.
b) e.g. –293°, –67°, 67°, 293°.
c) e.g. –269°, –89°, 91°, 271°.
(Remember answers are rounded — if you try working backwards to check them, they'll look wrong.)

Q5

	sine	cosine	tangent
a)	0.0872	–0.996	–0.0875
b)	–0.0872	–0.996	0.0875
c)	0.707	0.707	1
d)	–0.259	0.966	–0.268

e) For positive and negative values of the same sized angle, sine and tangent have one positive and one negative y-value. Cosine always has the same sign.
f) The cosine graph is symmetrical about the y-axis, so the positive and negative of any angle will give the same value. The other two graphs aren't symmetrical about the y-axis.

Loci and Constructions P.101-P.102

Q1

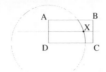

Not to scale

Q2

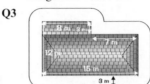

Not to scale

Length BA = 0.87 cm

Q3

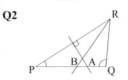

Not to scale

Q4

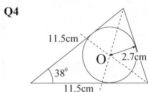

Not to scale
Radius of the circle = 2.7 cm

Q5 **a)** A circle with diameter AB.
b) and **c)**

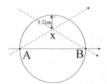

Not to scale

d) The ship comes 1.7 cm = 0.85 km from the rocks.

Q6

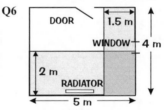

Not to scale

Q7 **a)**

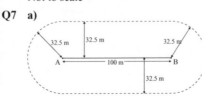

b) Distance around dashed path =
$(2 \times 100) + (\pi \times 65) = 404.2$ m

Q8

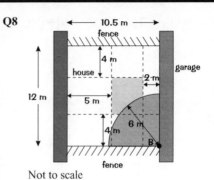

Not to scale

Q9 **a)**

b) Length = 8.6 cm equivalent to 43 km.
c) 35 km in 2.5 hrs, so speed
$= \frac{35}{2.5} = 14$ km/h.
d) and **e)** see diagram

Grouped Frequency Tables P.103

Q1 **a)**

Speed (km/h)	40≤s<45	45≤s<50	50≤s<55	55≤s<60	60≤s<65
Frequency	4	8	10	7	3
Mid-Interval	42.5	47.5	52.5	57.5	62.5
Frequency × Mid-Interval	170	380	525	402.5	187.5

Estimated mean = 52 km/h
(to nearest km/h)
b) 22 skiers   **c)** 20 skiers

Q2 **a)**

Weight (kg)	Tally	Frequency	Mid-Interval	Frequency × Mid-Interval
200 ≤ w < 250	IIII	4	225	900
250 ≤ w < 300	IIHT	5	275	1375
300 ≤ w < 350	IIHT II	7	325	2275
350 ≤ w < 400	II	2	375	750

b) 294 kg (to nearest kg)
c) 300 ≤ w < 350 kg

Q3 **a)**

Number	0≤n<0.2	0.2≤n<0.4	0.4≤n<0.6	0.6≤n<0.8	0.8≤n<1
Tally	HT HT II	HT I	HT HT II	HT HT	HT III
Frequency	12	6	12	10	8
Mid-Interval	0.1	0.3	0.5	0.7	0.9
Frequency × Mid-Interval	1.2	1.8	6	7	7.2

b) 0 ≤ n < 0.2 and 0.4 ≤ n < 0.6
c) 0.4 ≤ n < 0.6
d) 0.483 (3 dp)

Answers: P.104 — P.107

Cumulative Frequency P.104-P.105

Q1 accept:
a) 133-134 **c)** 136-137
b) 127-128 **d)** 8-10

Q2 **a)**

No. passengers	0≤n<50	50≤n<100	100≤n<150	150≤n<200	200≤n<250	250≤n<300
Frequency	2	7	10	5	3	1
Cumulative Frequency	2	9	19	24	27	28
Mid-Interval	25	75	125	175	225	275
Frequency × Mid-Interval	50	525	1250	875	675	275

Estimated mean = 130 passengers
(to nearest whole number)

b)

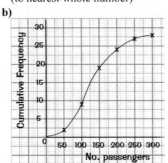

accept median of 118-122 passengers
c) 100 ≤ n < 150

Q3 **a)**

Mark (%)	0≤m<20	20≤m<40	40≤m<60	60≤m<80	80≤m<100
Frequency	2	12	18	5	3
Cumulative Frequency	2	14	32	37	40

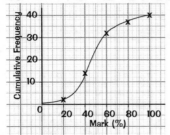

b) 36%-38%
c) 19%-21%
d) 45%-47%

Q4

Score	31≤s<41	41≤s<51	51≤s<61	61≤s<71	71≤s<81	81≤s<91	91≤s<101
Frequency	4	12	21	32	19	8	4
Cumulative Frequency	4	16	37	69	88	96	100

a) 61 ≤ s < 71
b) 61 ≤ s < 71
c)

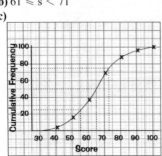

median = 65 (accept 64-66)
d) 73 – 55 = 18 (accept 17-19)

Q5 **a)**

Life (hours)	Frequency	Cumulative Frequency
900 ≤ L < 1000	10	10
1000 ≤ L < 1100	12	22
1100 ≤ L < 1200	15	37
1200 ≤ L < 1300	18	55
1300 ≤ L < 1400	22	77
1400 ≤ L < 1500	17	94
1500 ≤ L < 1600	14	108
1600 ≤ L < 1700	9	117

b) 1300 ≤ L < 1400
c)

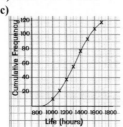

median = 1320 hours (±20)
d) lower quartile = 1150 (±20)
upper quartile = 1460 (±20)

Q6 **a)**

Time	2:00≤t<2:30	2:30≤t<3:00	3:00≤t<3:30	3:30≤t<4:00	4:00≤t<4:30
Tally	I	IIHT	IIHT IIHT IIII	IIHT II	III
Frequency	1	5	14	7	3
Cumulative Frequency	1	6	20	27	30

b)

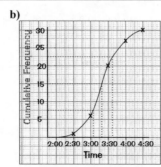

c) median = 3:19 (±3)
upper quartile = 3:37 (±3)
lower quartile = 3:05 (±3)
d) 0:32 (±5)

Histograms and Frequency Density P.106-P.107

Q1 4 × 10 = 40 people

Q2 **a)**

Weight (kg)	0≤w<2	2≤w<4	4≤w<7	7≤w<9	9≤w<15
Frequency	3	2	6	9	12
Frequency density	1.5	1	2	4.5	2

b)

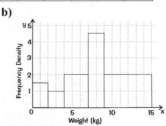

c) 23 hives

Q3 (A,I), (B,II)

Q4 **a)**

No. of hours	Frequency	Frequency density
0 ≤ h < 1	6	6
1 ≤ h < 3	13	6.5
3 ≤ h < 5	15	7.5
5 ≤ h < 8	9	3
8 ≤ h < 10	23	11.5
10 ≤ h < 15	25	5
15 ≤ h < 20	12	2.4

b) 103 students
c)

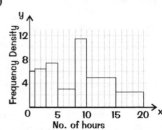

d) 41 students

Q5 A — 16 year olds

B — bags of sugar

Q6 **a)**

Salary (£1000s)	0 ≤ x < 10	10 ≤ x < 20	20 ≤ x < 30	30 ≤ x < 40	40 ≤ x < 50
Frequency	10	25	42	20	3
Frequency Density	1	2.5	4.2	2	0.3

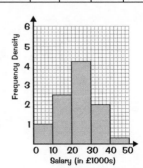

b) E.g. there are more people with higher salaries now than 10 years ago.

Answers: P.108

Scatter Diagrams P.108

Q1   (A,S), (B,R), (C,P), (D,U)

Q2   **a)**

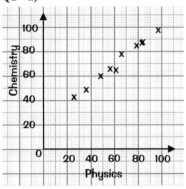

   b) Strong positive correlation.
   c) Yes

Q3   **a), b)**

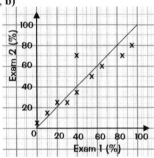

   c) 50%

Q4   **a), b)**

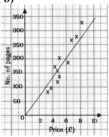

   c) £7.50 (±20p)

ISBN 978 1 84762 465 9

9 781847 624659

MWHA41